THE GREAT
ART SCANDAL

ANNA NILSEN

KINGFISHER

BOSTON

For Tomas & Peter
and
Pat & Heidi
from ATB

KINGFISHER

a Houghton Mifflin Company imprint
222 Berkeley Street
Boston, Massachusetts 02116
www.houghtonmifflinbooks.com

First published in 2003
2 4 6 8 10 9 7 5 3 1
1TR/0602/WKT/CLSN(CLSN)/157SPKC2S

Concept © Anna Nilsen
Copyright © Kingfisher Publications Plc 2003

Exhibition Artwork: Anna Nilsen
Illustrator: Martha Gavin
Author and Managing Editor: Russell Mclean
Coordinating Editor: Stephanie Pliakas
Senior Designer: Jane Tassie
Picture Research: Christine Thompson, Cecilia Weston-Baker
DTP Coordinator: Sarah Pfitzner
DTP Operator: Primrose Burton
Production Controller: Debbie Otter
Consultant: Elaine Ward

LIBRARY OF CONGRESS CATALOGING-IN-PUBLICATION DATA
Nilsen, Anna, 1948–
The great art scandal/Anna Nilsen—1st ed.
p. cm.
Summary: Introduces 20th-century art through 32 paintings by 16 artists,
within which are hidden details taken from the works of such masters as Currie, Seurat,
Hockney, and Lichtenstein.
1. Painting, Modern—20th century—Juvenile literature. 2. Picture puzzles—Juvenile
literature. [1. Painting, Modern—20th century. 2. Art appreciation. 3. Picture puzzles.]
I. Title.
ND1146.N55 2003
759.06—dc21   2003040062

ISBN 0-7534-5587-0

Printed in Hong Kong

The Publishers would like to thank the following for permission to reproduce their material. Every care has been taken to trace copyright holders. However, if there have been unintentional omissions or failure to trace copyright holders, we apologize and will, if informed, endeavor to make corrections in any future edition.

All paintings (with the exception of *Dauphinée House* by Edward Hopper and *Bather and Sand Castle* by Sidney Nolan) reproduced courtesy of the Trustees of the National Galleries of Scotland.

© **National Gallery of Scotland**: Cézanne, Paul, NG 2236; Constable, John, NG 2016; Degas, Edgar, NG 2225; Gauguin, Paul, NG 1643; van Gogh, Vincent, NG 1803; Monet, Claude, NG 2399; Seurat, Georges, NG 2222.

© **Scottish National Portrait Gallery**: Bellany, John, PG 2888, © the artist; Colvin, Calum, © the artist, PGP 83.14.

© **Scottish National Gallery of Modern Art**:
Auerbach, Frank, GMA 1537, © courtesy of Marlborough Fine Art; Cadell, Francis Campbell Boileau, GMA 3350, © the Portland Gallery; Currie, Ken, GMA 3012A, © the artist; Davie, Alan, GMA 4113, © the artist; Eardley, Joan, GMA 887, © the artist's estate; Frost, Terry, GMA 1299, © the artist; Gilbert & George, GMA 2507, © the artists; Goncharova, Natalya GMA 796; Hockney, David, GMA 1538, © the artist; Kirchner, Ernst Ludwig, GMA 911, © Dr Wolfgang & Ingeborg Henze-Ketterer, Wichtrach/Bern; Lewis, Wyndham, GMA 1685, © the artist's estate; Lichtenstein, Roy, GMA 2133; Nash, Paul, GMA 774, © Tate, London, 2003; Nicholson, Winifred, GMA 2964, © the Trustees of Winifred Nicholson; Nolde, Emil, GMA 1082, © Nolde-Stiftung Seebüll; Penrose, Roland, GMA 4070, © A. & R. Penrose; Piper, John, GMA 1998, © the artist's estate; Pollock, Jackson, GMA 2198; Redpath, Anne, GMA 932, © the Bridgeman Art Library; Sutherland, Graham, GMA 1072, © the artist's estate; Tanguy, Yves, GMA 4084; Warhol, Andy, GMA 4095.

We would also like to thank the Design and Artists Copyright Society for their kind permission to reproduce the artists listed below. Artists represented by DACS: Natalya Goncharova © ADAGP, Paris/DACS, London 2003; Roy Lichtenstein © The Estate of Roy Lichtenstein/DACS 2003; Claude Monet © ADAGP, Paris and DACS, London 2003; Jackson Pollock © ARS, NY and DACS, London 2003; Yves Tanguy © ARS, NY and DACS, London 2003; Andy Warhol © The Andy Warhol Foundation for the Visual Arts, Inc./ ARS, NY and DACS, London 2003.

We would also like to thank the Bridgeman Art Library for their kind permission to reproduce the artists listed below. Artists represented by Bridgeman Art Library: Hopper, Edward; Nolan, Sir Sidney.

THE BREAK-IN

Luckily I found this press release on the floor of my office. Take a close look because it will help you figure out which artist painted each picture.

Inspiration City

An exhibition of 32 new paintings inspired by the modern art masterpieces of the City Gallery

THE CITY GALLERY
OCTOBER 1—JANUARY 31

EYE TEAM 👁

Name: Baxter Ball
Number of details: 2

Name: Belinda Blinker
Number of details: 3

Name: Pedro Pupilio
Number of details: 4

Name: Iris Brown
Number of details: 5

SPIDER TEAM 🕷

Name: Win Widow
Number of details: 2

Name: Tyler Trapdoor
Number of details: 3

Name: Celia Webb
Number of details: 4

Name: Randall Redback
Number of details: 5

To celebrate the tenth anniversary of the City Gallery 16 world-famous artists have each created two new paintings, making a total of 32 pictures. The artists have been divided into four teams. Each team stamps its work with one particular symbol hidden somewhere in the painting.

The exhibits have been inspired by the pictures in the City Gallery's collection. Each artist has used two, three, four, or five details from these modern art masterpieces. For example, the two paintings by Celia Webb both contain four details, as well as her team symbol—a spider.

PLANET TEAM 🪐

Name: Sami Saturn
Number of details: 2

Name: Pluto Moon
Number of details: 3

Name: Vernon Venus
Number of details: 4

Name: Hans van Mars
Number of details: 5

HEART TEAM ♥

Name: Petula Pulse
Number of details: 2

Name: Beat Basham
Number of details: 3

Name: Cherry Chambers
Number of details: 4

Name: Victor Vessel
Number of details: 5

THE ROGUE PAINTING

But Molly's morning is about to go from bad to worse . . .

Molly, you'd better read this letter. It arrived late last night from one of the artists.

To Molly Adams,

Please read this letter carefully—it could save you and your gallery from disaster. Take a very close look at the 32 paintings in the exhibition. Maxwell Garrett, the owner of the Masters Gallery, has bribed one of my fellow artists to sabotage your show. One painting contains a detail taken without permission from a famous work in Garrett's collection. If you exhibit this painting tonight, he will sue the City Gallery for millions of dollars.

How do I know this? Well, I've suspected that Garrett has been up to no good for some time, so I've been doing some detective work. But now I think he may be on to me, so for my own safety I'm keeping my identity a secret. It's up to you to find the rogue painting and remove it from the exhibition.

To help you here's a copy of the painting in Garrett's collection.

Good luck.

This is the most famous picture in the Masters Gallery—*The Vale of Dedham*, painted in 1828 by English artist John Constable. You will need to examine it very carefully. If you can't find the rogue painting that includes a detail from this picture, Garrett will sue. That could mean the end of the City Gallery— and my career.

LOOK FOR THE CLUES!

Time's running out, but if you can determine who made the paintings in the exhibition and spot the rogue picture, we could be saved. Here comes Mr. Dempsey for our meeting—it's time to start your detective work!

A piece of paper and a pencil will come in handy. You should also take the City Gallery Catalog with you (turn to page 9)—it contains photos of all the artwork in our collection. Remember, the artists in the new exhibition have used details from these works to create their new paintings.

THE CITY GALLERY
CATALOG

Enter the exhibition of new paintings on page 9. The bottom section of the page is the catalog of the City Gallery's collection. The paintings in the exhibition are made up of details from the works in the catalog, which is arranged in alphabetical order according to the last name of the artist. Let's start by looking at the first painting in the show.

First you need to identify which team the painting belongs to. I've found a spider! So this picture has been painted by an artist in the spider team. I can also see that the artist has used details from three paintings. The wrestling figures are taken from Paul Gauguin, the man sitting down is from Georges Seurat, and the rest of the painting is taken from Winifred Nicholson.

MPLATION

Now turn back to the press release. By matching the spider symbol with three details I can work out that this painting was made by Tyler Trapdoor.

Inspiration City

An exhibition of 32 new paintings inspired by
modern art masterpieces of the City Gallery

THE CITY GALLERY
OCTOBER 1–JANUARY 31

Name: Belinda Blinker
Number of details: 3

Name: Pedro Pupilo
Number of details: 4

Name: Iris Brown
Number of details: 5

Name: Tyler Trap
Number of detail

Name: Randall Redback
Number of details: 5

HEART

Name: Petula Pulse
Number of details: 2

On your piece of paper draw a chart like this. Fill in the title of each painting and the name of the artist who painted it as you go through the exhibition. Remember, one of the paintings contains a detail from *The Vale of Dedham* by John Constable—if you find it, write its title and who painted it in the bottom section.

TEAM SYMBOL / NUMBER OF DETAILS	EYE TEAM 👁	SPIDER TEAM 🕷	PLANET TEAM 🪐	HEART TEAM ♥
2				
3		CONTEMPLATION Tyler Trapdoor		
4				
5				
ROGUE PAINTING				

Your mission is to . . .

1. Figure out who made each painting so that new labels can be made before the exhibition opens. (Remember, every artist has made two paintings.)

2. Spot the rogue painting in time for it to be removed from the exhibition.

GOOD LUCK!

If you need some help, turn to page 45.
The answers are on pages 46–48—but don't cheat!

THE CITY GALLERY
CATALOG

E. O. W. IV 1961

Oil paint on plywood 23 in. x 22 in.

Born in Germany, Frank Auerbach was sent to Great Britain by his parents when World War II broke out. He has lived in London, England, since the mid-1940s.

Auerbach paints the same close friends and London scenes over and over again. He made many portraits of his partner, Estella Olive West, whom he called E. O. W. Like many of his works, the paint on *E.O.W. IV* is thick and heavily textured. Some portraits of West took hundreds of sittings to complete. After several hours of work Auerbach would scrape away almost all of the paint, leaving the ghost of an image as a starting point for the next session. Eventually Auerbach would be happy with the portrait.

For many years Auerbach painted in monochrome (shades of one color)—partly to save money but also because of the influence of the Dutch painter Rembrandt. From the mid-1960s he could afford brighter paints, and his pictures became much more colorful.

JOHN **BELLANY** born 1942 **U.K.**

Sir Peter Maxwell Davies 1991

Oil paint on canvas 67 in. x 59 in.

John Bellany was born into a family of fishermen on the east coast of Scotland. Many of his paintings contain images of fish, seabirds, and boats, but he is also well-known for his portraits.

This large painting shows British classical composer Sir Peter Maxwell Davies. When the two men first met, Bellany was struck by Maxwell Davies' piercing black eyes. In the portrait the composer's eyes form a calm center. Around his head swirl vibrant reds, yellows, and blues (the three primary colors), painted with energetic brush strokes. They suggest that Maxwell Davies is a creative and charismatic composer, full of exciting, colorful ideas.

The word "Max"—written on the scrap of paper in Maxwell Davies' hand—may simply be the first part of the composer's last name, or it could be a clue to one of Bellany's favorite painters, the German expressionist Max Beckmann. Like Bellany, Beckmann painted with intense colors and dynamic brush strokes.

FRANCIS CAMPBELL BOILEAU **CADELL** 1883–1937 **U.K.**

Portrait of a Lady in Black around 1921

Oil paint on canvas 30 in. x 25 in.

Cadell was born in Edinburgh, Scotland, but first trained as a painter in Paris, France, between 1899 and 1902. There he admired the work of impressionist painters such as Claude Monet and Edgar Degas. When he returned to Scotland, Cadell continued to paint in the impressionist style. After World War I he moved away from impressionism by experimenting with strong, geometric shapes.

Portrait of a Lady in Black is one of Cadell's early paintings in this style. The shadows are very light, and the brush strokes are almost invisible, making the portrait appear almost as a pattern of two-dimensional, or flat, shapes.

The elegant woman in the picture is Berthia Hamilton Don-Wachaupe, a model who lived in Edinburgh and posed many times for Cadell between 1911 and 1926. Portraits often show her wearing a black hat, and although she looks much younger, she would have been almost 60 when this painting was made. The distinctive mauve walls suggest that Cadell painted the work in his Edinburgh studio.

PAUL **CÉZANNE**   1839–1906 **France**

Sainte-Victoire Mountain 1890s

Oil paint on canvas 21 in. x 25 in.

Cézanne began his career as an impressionist painter in Paris, France, in the 1860s. But he soon developed a style of his own and moved back to his hometown of Aix-en-Provence in the south of France. There Cézanne liked to paint the same scenes over and over again. Instead of simply copying what he saw, he was trying to understand the patterns and shapes at the heart of nature. Because of his unusual way of looking at a subject, Cézanne has been called the father of modern art.

Cézanne's favorite subject was the local Sainte-Victoire mountain, which he painted many times. Unlike the impressionists, Cézanne worked slowly and used a small range of colors to capture the solidity of a landscape. In this picture he deliberately left patches of bare canvas to highlight the vibrancy of the blues, greens, and yellows.

CALUM **COLVIN** born 1961 **U.K.**

James MacMillan 1996

Cibachrome photograph 60 in. x 48 in.

Calum Colvin has a unique style that mixes sculpture, painting, and photography. To create this large portrait of the Scottish composer James MacMillan Colvin carefully arranged pieces of furniture and other objects in the corner of a room. Some of these items are clues to the composer's work and interests—music sheets and instruments, pieces from the stage set of an opera that MacMillan had written, religious paintings, and a pair of tickets to a soccer game. Other objects form parts of the sitter's face—the back of a chair becomes his jaw, for example.

MacMillan's other features have been painted onto the walls, the table, and the seat of the chair. When the whole thing is photographed from a particular point, an optical illusion is created. The separate lines join, and the colors merge together to form an image of the composer's head, standing out from the real objects onto which it is painted.

In the final photograph MacMillan's head is at the center of a busy scene, suggesting that the composer has many influences and interests, as well as an energetic and creative mind.

KEN **CURRIE**   born 1960   **U.K.**

Template of the Future 1986

Oil paint on canvas 84 in. x 106 in.

Ken Currie lives and works in the Scottish city of Glasgow. Many of his pictures tell the story of how industrial workers in Glasgow struggled against poverty during the 1900s.

Template of the Future is a dark and detailed painting. In the top right corner an old man sits in a bar telling the younger man opposite him about his days as a shipbuilder in the Glasgow docks. His words come to life, and in the foreground we see the storyteller as a younger man sitting in the docks with his son on his shoulders. Behind him welders and riveters are hard at work welding together huge sheets of steel. The browns and oranges in this picture recreate the hot, gloomy conditions in which the shipbuilders worked.

ALAN **DAVIE**   born 1920 **U.K.**

Lush Life 1961

Oil paint on canvas 83 in. x 67 in.

The jewellike shapes and the title of *Lush Life* hint at the glowing flowers and fruits of the great Dutch still-life paintings of the 1500s and 1600s. The artist, Alan Davie, was also inspired by abstract expressionist painters from the U.S., whose work he first saw at an exhibition in Venice, Italy, in 1948. By the early 1950s Davie was painting in a style similar to that of Jackson Pollock. He would place the canvas flat on the floor and apply strong, heavy brush strokes, with no plan of what the finished work would look like.

By the time he painted *Lush Life* in 1961 Davie was planning his pictures more carefully, but this enormous abstract piece is still overflowing with energy and life. The vibrant shapes and colors explosively burst out from the center of the painting. Like other abstract expressionist artists, Davie is trying to express his feelings directly through the paint. We cannot say for certain what those feelings are, but the rich colors and sense of movement suggest that he felt full of energy and optimism when he worked on this piece.

EDGAR **DEGAS**   1834–1917 **France**

A Group of Dancers 1890s

Oil paint on paper laid on canvas   18 in. x 24 in.

The impressionist artist Edgar Degas loved ballet— more than 1,500 of his paintings, drawings, and pastel sketches of dancers survive today. They look fresh and lively because he made most of them on the spot.

Degas was fascinated by the way the human body moves. In this painting of three ballerinas in front of a rehearsal room mirror flowing curves and diagonal lines capture the graceful motion of the dancers. We can see, however, that Degas was not interested in the dancers as individuals because their faces are blurred and featureless. The ballerina on the far right is cut off by the edge of the picture. Degas borrowed this technique from Japanese prints, which were popular in Europe during the late 1800s.

JOAN **EARDLEY** 1921–1963 **U.K.**

Street Kids around 1949–1951

Oil paint on canvas 40 in. x 29 in.

Born in southern England, Joan Eardley moved to the large Scottish city of Glasgow in the late 1930s. She was deeply affected by the life and atmosphere of the slums, or poor areas, of the city. The local children who played outside Eardley's studio were favorite subjects during her time in Glasgow— adults rarely appear in her paintings.

Street Kids is a study of three children sitting on the sidewalk. A girl reads a comic book, a boy in an orange sweater eats an apple, while a second boy rests against the wall. The children are poor, but the warm colors and their relaxed poses tell us that they are close friends or maybe even members of the same family.

Shortly after painting Street Kids Eardley moved to a small fishing village on the east coast of Scotland. There she painted the village, the harbor, and the sea in all types of weather and in many different moods. She usually worked outside and often mixed sand and pieces of grass into her paints. These gave her work more texture, almost as if the fierce winter wind of the Scottish coast had blown the particles on to the wet canvas.

TERRY **FROST** born 1915 **U.K.**

Black and White Movement on Blue and Green II 1951–1952

Oil paint on canvas 44 in. x 34 in.

Terry Frost began painting when he was a prisoner of war in Germany during World War II. He is one of Great Britain's best-known abstract painters. Abstract artists do not try to show their subject realistically. They use colors and shapes—as well as their imagination—to give an idea of what something is like or to express their feelings about the subject. Some abstract art, called "nonrepresentational," is made up of shapes and colors that do not depict anything at all.

Black and White Movement on Blue and Green II was inspired by the boats moored in the harbor of St. Ives, a town in southern England. The painting is full of life and movement. Crescent-shaped hulls bob up and down with the blue-green waves, while the triangular shapes look like masts and sails. This was Frost's second attempt to capture the emotions he felt sitting by the harbor. An earlier, slightly different version of this vibrant painting hangs in the Tate Gallery in London, England.

PAUL **GAUGUIN** 1848–1903 **France**

**The Vision after the Sermon
(Jacob and the Angel)** 1888

Oil paint on canvas 28 in. x 36 in.

Paul Gauguin was one of the first postimpressionist painters. He used glowing, flat colors and filled his pictures with hidden meanings. In this scene a group of French villagers has just heard the Old Testament story of how Jacob spent a whole night wrestling with a mysterious angel. As the women pray the fight comes to life in their minds. Gauguin contrasts the natural poses of the villagers with the unnatural colors and perspective of the events taking place in their imaginations.

In 1891 Gauguin moved to the Pacific island of Tahiti. There he created his best-known work, depicting the islanders in bright, startling colors. Although Gauguin is very famous today, he died in poverty and was unknown to the public.

GILBERT & GEORGE born 1943 and 1942 **U.K.**

Exhausted 1980

16 photographs, dyed and framed 94 in. x 79 in.

Italian-born Gilbert Proesch and Englishman George Passmore met in 1967 when they were both art students in London, England. They decided to give up their last names and turn their lives into one long work of art. Throughout their career Gilbert & George have rejected the traditional techniques of painting and sculpture. For their early pieces the pair transformed themselves into "living sculptures." Dressed in business suits, with their faces painted silver, they would repeat the same stylized actions hour after hour.

Since the late 1970s Gilbert & George have been making brightly tinted black-and-white prints of themselves. Photographs are printed, dyed, and framed one by one and then joined to make giant "photo sculptures." The self-portrait *Exhausted* is one example, showing Gilbert above and George below. The deliberately childlike black portrait drawings stand out boldly from the 16 sheets of yellow paper on which they are printed. As with many of Gilbert & George's works the sheer size of the portraits heightens their impact.

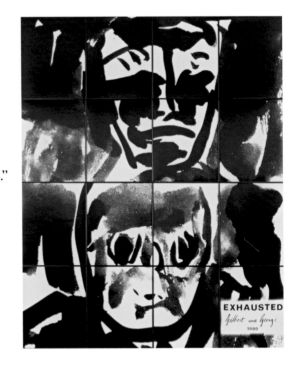

EXHAUSTED
Gilbert and George
1980

VINCENT VAN **GOGH** 1853–1890 **Netherlands**

Olive Trees 1889

Oil paint on canvas 20 in. x 25 in.

Van Gogh was a postimpressionist painter. He sold only one painting during his lifetime, yet today he is considered to be one of the world's greatest artists. Van Gogh lived in poverty and suffered attacks of mental illness. In 1888 he famously cut off part of his left ear.

At the time he painted *Olive Trees* van Gogh was living in a mental institution in Saint-Rémy in the south of France. The struggle to capture the ever-changing colors of the trees and the earth under the hot sun became his obsession—he painted at least 14 pictures of olive groves during his year at the institution. The swirling, energetic brush strokes reveal van Gogh's turbulent state of mind at this time. One year after painting *Olive Trees* he killed himself at the age of 37.

NATALYA **GONCHAROVA** 1881–1962 **Russia**

Rabbi with Cat around 1912

Oil paint on canvas 39 in. x 36 in.

Goncharova was a leading member of a Russian avant-garde art movement that was based in Moscow in the early 1900s. From 1917 she lived and worked in Paris, France, with her lifelong companion, the artist Mikhail Larionov. As well as painting, Goncharova became famous for designing innovative sets and costumes for ballets and plays.

Rabbi with Cat is painted in a deliberately childlike style that reflects Goncharova's admiration of "primitive" Russian folk art and religious pictures. The man holding the cat is a rabbi, or Jewish teacher. Millions of Jews lived in Russia in the early 1900s. They suffered persecution and were even the victims of vicious gang attacks, known as pogroms. The two men in the background are Jews fleeing from a pogrom with their belongings slung over their backs. In the top left corner is the Hand of God blessing the rabbi. The rabbi may be stroking his cat for the last time before he also tries to escape.

DAVID **HOCKNEY**   born 1937 **U.K.**

Rocky Mountains and Tired Indians 1965

Acrylic paint on canvas 66 in. x 99 in.

David Hockney is one of the most famous British painters alive today. He has lived and worked in Los Angeles, California, since the 1960s.

Hockney painted *Rocky Mountains and Tired Indians* while he was teaching at a university in Colorado at the foot of the Rocky Mountains. His studio had no windows, so he invented the scene from magazine photographs and his own imagination. The blue chair gives the painting balance, and to explain its presence Hockney called the Native Americans, or Indians, "tired."

EDWARD **HOPPER** 1882–1967 **U.S.**

Dauphinée House 1932

Oil paint on canvas   34 in. x 50 in.

Edward Hopper is one of America's best-known artists, famous for his paintings of New York City and small New England towns. He painted ordinary scenes with great realism—city streets and country roads, houses, restaurants, storefronts, and bedrooms. Hopper was particularly skilled at creating atmosphere through his use of light and shadows. In *Dauphinée House* a typical New England home is captured at dusk. The soft, fading sunlight illuminates the white walls of the building against the darkening silhouettes of trees and bushes. The scene has no people in it, adding to the sense of stillness and melancholy.

ERNST LUDWIG **KIRCHNER** 1880–1938 **Germany**

Japanese Theater around 1909

Oil paint on canvas 44 in. x 44 in.

Kirchner was a member of a group of expressionist artists from Dresden, Germany, known as "Die Brücke," or the Bridge Group. He was influenced by the bright colors of African and Polynesian art, as well as by Japanese prints and the paintings of van Gogh and Gauguin.

Theater, cabaret, and the circus were very popular in Germany in the early 1900s. Kirchner loved to paint the exotic actors, singers, dancers, acrobats, and wrestlers who performed in the theaters and bars of Dresden. He used intense colors, jagged shapes, and strong brush strokes to fill his pictures with life. This painting shows a performance by a company of Japanese actors. The two women in the foreground look as if they are about to step off the front of the stage. Behind them a figure in red stands beneath a richly decorated curtain. The play may be about to reach its dramatic climax—the woman on the left seems to be holding a dagger, poised to strike.

WYNDHAM **LEWIS** 1882–1957 **U.K.**

A Reading of Ovid (Tyros) 1920–1921

Oil paint on canvas 64 in. x 35 in.

Wyndham Lewis was born in Canada, but he moved to Great Britain with his family in 1888. He studied painting in London, and in 1914, inspired by cubist painters such as Picasso, he founded an art movement called vorticism. As well as painting, he wrote many novels, poems, and plays. People were often shocked by his work—Lewis had strong opinions about art, politics, and literature, and he was not afraid to criticize other writers and artists.

Between 1920 and 1921 Lewis painted a series of portraits of "tyros." "Tyro" means novice or beginner, but Lewis used the word in a slightly different way. His tyros are people who paint, read, or write with a lot of energy and enthusiasm but without truly understanding what they are doing. The two tyros in this picture are studying the poems of the ancient Roman poet Ovid. Painted in bold colors and sharp lines, the grinning, masklike faces of the two men leap out at the viewer. At first glance the students seem to be enjoying the poems, but their unnatural smiles reveal how uncomfortable they really feel. Lewis was making fun of people who began writing, painting, and studying literature simply because these were fashionable activities in the 1920s.

ROY **LICHTENSTEIN**   1923–1997 **U.S.**

In the Car 1963

Oil paint and magna on canvas 67 in. x 80 in.

Roy Lichtenstein was one of a group of painters and sculptors known as pop artists who burst on to the scene in the 1960s. They were inspired by the color and energy of a new, popular culture of fast food, fast cars, color televisions, advertising, fashion, movies, and popular music.

Lichtenstein especially loved comic strips. He copied the bright, eye-catching colors that leap out at the viewer, as well as the dots of the printing process that make up the images. Like many of his works, *In the Car* is a huge painting based on just one frame from a comic strip. We don't know the whole story, so we have to guess what is happening. Are the couple married, or have they just met? Where are they going, and why are they driving so fast? These questions add to the drama and excitement of the scene.

CLAUDE **MONET**   1840–1926 **France**

A Seascape, Shipping by Moonlight   1860s

Oil paint on canvas 23 in. x 29 in.

Monet was one of the founding members of the impressionist group of painters. These artists tried to capture the effect of light on objects and landscapes. Because light changes so rapidly, the impressionists had to work quickly, using loose strokes of color to create a snapshot—or impression—of a moment in time. Although very popular now, people were puzzled when they first saw the work of the impressionists—they thought the paintings looked rough and unfinished.

This moonlit view of the harbor in Honfleur in northern France is one of Monet's early paintings. As well as a brush, Monet used a flexible palette knife to lay the paint thickly onto the canvas, helping him create a very bold lighting effect that adds to the dramatic atmosphere.

PAUL **NASH** 1889–1946 **U.K.**

Landscape of the Vernal Equinox (III) 1944

Oil paint on canvas 25 in. x 30 in.

Throughout his career Paul Nash painted in many different styles. He experimented with surrealism and abstract art in the 1930s. During both world wars he worked for the British government as a war artist.

Like many of Nash's later paintings, this gentle, dreamlike landscape is full of hidden meanings. It focuses on two tree-covered mounds near Oxford in southern England. Nash first painted them in 1912 and was fascinated by the mystery and magic of the setting ever since. The scene depicts the vernal (spring) equinox when day and night are the same length. At the time Nash knew that he did not have long to live, and the positions of the Sun and Moon reflect his failing health—as the Sun sets its warm, pink glow is replaced by the colder, blue light of the rising Moon.

WINIFRED **NICHOLSON** 1893–1981 **U.K.**

Jake and Kate on the Isle of Wight 1931–1932

Oil paint on canvas 27 in. x 35 in.

Winifred Nicholson was one of the most popular British artists from the 1900s. She often painted flowers and landscapes in delicate, fresh colors.

Nicholson spent the winter of 1931–1932 on the Isle of Wight off the coast of southern England with her three children, Jake, Kate, and Andrew. This picture depicts Jake and Kate sitting in a conservatory overlooking the sea. Their fancy hats show that it may be Christmas. Until recently the title of the painting was *Jake, Kate, and the Normandie* because the large ship in the distance was believed to be a French cruise liner with that name. In fact, the *Normandie* was not launched until 1935. The liner may be a German ship, or it may have been invented by Nicholson.

SIDNEY **NOLAN** 1917–1992 **Australia**

Bather and Sand Castle 1945

Ripolin paint on cardboard 25 in. x 30 in.

Sidney Nolan worked as a bicycle racer, a cook, and a gold miner before becoming an artist at the age of 21. He had little training and soon developed a very personal style of painting. Many of his works capture the brilliant blue skies and fierce heat of the sun-baked Australian outback, but he is best known for his paintings of the notorious 19th-century gangster Ned Kelly.

In the 1940s Nolan painted a series of pictures of people at the beach. These captured the carefree antics of his childhood days in St. Kilda, a seaside resort near his hometown of Melbourne. *Bather and Sand Castle* is painted in a deliberately childlike way. The deep blue sky and rich yellow sand glow with warmth and conjure up happy memories of sun-soaked vacations at the beach.

EMIL **NOLDE**   1867–1956 **Germany**

Head 1913

Oil paint on canvas 30 in. x 26 in.

Emil Nolde belonged to a group of artists known as the expressionists. They worked in northern Europe in the early 1900s, inspired by the work of van Gogh and Gauguin. At the time many people were shocked by the crude but powerful way in which these artists painted. Instead of depicting how objects really looked, the expressionists used painting as a way to express how they felt about modern life. Many of their pictures show crowded scenes painted in heavy, jagged lines and jarring colors.

This mysterious portrait of an unknown woman reveals Nolde's fascination with primitive African art. The woman's face looks like a tribal mask with angular lines and a blank expression. Her intense turquoise shirt leaps out harshly against the dull, reddish-brown background. The overall effect is unsettling—we don't know who the woman is, and her severe, lifeless face gives us few clues about what she was really like. Shortly after painting *Head* Nolde's interest in primitive art led him to join a year-long expedition to New Guinea.

Untitled 1937

Collage, gouache, and pencil on cardboard 32 in. x 21 in.

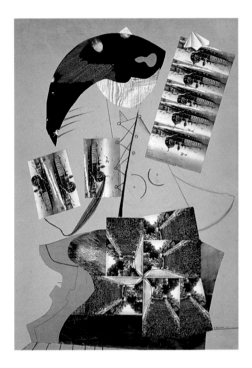

Between 1922 and 1935 the British painter, poet, and sculptor Roland Penrose lived in Paris, France. There he became closely involved with the surrealist group of artists. In 1936 Penrose introduced surrealism to Great Britain by organizing a very successful exhibition in London.

This untitled work is a collage—a picture made by combining painting and drawing with other materials stuck onto a surface. Newspaper, photographs, and scraps of cloth are some of the most popular materials, but a collage can be made of almost anything. Penrose loved the vivid colors of the postcards that he bought on his travels. He found that clusters of the same image could take on the form of a spread of feathers or the petals of a flower. The shapes in this collage look like a human form or a machine—or even a combination of the two. A black-haired head seems to sit on a pencil-drawn body, while the blue seaside postcards on either side of the body look like a pair of arms. The cluster of red postcards at the bottom give the picture a sense of movement—they could be a spinning motor or a pair of fast-moving legs!

JOHN **PIPER** 1903–1992 **U.K.**

Black Ground 1938

Oil paint on canvas 48 in. x 71 in.

John Piper is best known for his landscape pictures, but for a period in the 1930s he created abstract works such as *Black Ground*. This painting was inspired by an avant-garde art movement called cubism, which was developed by the artists Pablo Picasso and Georges Braque around 1907. Like many cubist works, *Black Ground* is difficult to understand at first. On the left side of the picture are a stringed instrument and a bottle, but their shapes are broken into angular blocks of color. The cubists painted in this way because they wanted to change the idea that artists should only copy exactly what they see with their eyes.

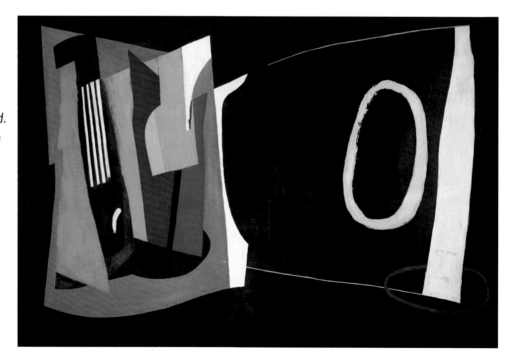

JACKSON **POLLOCK**   1912–1956 **U.S.**

Untitled around 1946

Oil paint, pen and ink, and watercolor on paper   20 in. x 13 in.

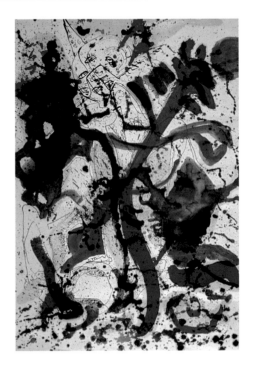

During World War II many artists left Europe for the U.S. Their ideas about cubism, surrealism, and abstract art inspired American artists, such as Jackson Pollock, to develop a new art movement. It became known as abstract expressionism.

Pollock was the most famous abstract expressionist. He tried to express his innermost feelings through painting and developed a new technique called "drip painting," which allowed him to work quickly and with little planning. Pollock would lay the canvas on the floor and pour paint straight onto the surface from a can. With sticks, knives, and trowels he would spread and drip the paint across the canvas, creating a jumble of twisting lines and colors.

Many of Pollock's drip paintings are huge, but *Untitled* is a small work on paper created when Pollock was first developing his new technique. It is not entirely abstract—toward the top you can make out a rough human figure drawn in black ink. Like many of Pollock's paintings, the picture fizzes with life, energy, and movement.

ANNE **REDPATH** 1895–1965 **U.K.**

The Indian Rug around 1942

Oil paint on plywood 29 in. x 37 in.

Anne Redpath studied painting in Edinburgh, Scotland, between 1913 and 1919 before moving to France, where she raised a family. Her career as an artist did not take off until she returned to Scotland in 1934.

Like many of Redpath's pictures, *The Indian Rug* is a still life—a painting of a group of static objects. The exotic rug was inspired by the patterned textiles designed by Redpath's father, while the vivid reds, blues, and yellow reflect the artist's admiration for the French painter Henri Matisse. Redpath was interested in creating patterns in her work. The "real" objects in this picture—such as the chair and the slippers— deliberately appear as flat areas of color that merge with the two-dimensional birds and trees on the rug.

GEORGES **SEURAT**   1859–1891   **France**

A Study for "Bathers at Asnières" early 1880s

Oil paint on wood 6 in. x 6 in.

Seurat was a French postimpressionist painter. This is one of 13 oil sketches that he made to help him figure out the composition of a much larger picture called *Bathers at Asnières*. In the final painting a swimming factory worker takes the place of the horse being washed in the river, and several more people and a dog are added to the riverbank.

Later in his life Seurat developed an important technique called pointillism, using dots of unmixed paint to create an overall effect of vibrant color.

GRAHAM **SUTHERLAND** 1903–1980 **U.K.**

Western Hills 1938/1941

Oil paint on canvas 22 in. x 36 in.

Sutherland was a lover of nature who began his career as a printmaker, specializing in etchings of English fields and cottages. He only began painting in his late 20s. The wild, bare scenery of Pembrokeshire in Wales inspired many of Sutherland's haunting landscapes, including *Western Hills*. First made in 1938, Sutherland repainted this picture three years later, heightening its dramatic impact. Beneath the rich glow of the setting sun the ominous stony outcrops seem to be on fire, detailed in brilliant pinks and oranges.

YVES **TANGUY** 1900–1955 **France/U.S.**

The Ribbon of Excess 1932

Oil paint on wood 14 in. x 18 in.

In 1923 Yves Tanguy was riding on a bus in Paris, France, when he caught sight of two paintings by the Italian artist Giorgio de Chirico in an art gallery window. He decided there and then to become a painter—even though he had no artistic training. Tanguy joined a group of artists known as the surrealists, who painted dreamlike pictures full of strange objects.

The Ribbon of Excess is packed full of precise, beanlike shapes that cast long shadows over an eerie landscape. A large cloud of smoke or dust suggests a battle in the desert or even in another world. No one knows the real meaning of the picture or even if it means anything at all—Tanguy once said that his paintings, like dreams, could not and should not be explained.

ANDY **WARHOL** 1928–1987 **U.S.**

Portrait of Maurice 1976

Oil paint and silk-screen print on canvas 26 in. x 32 in.

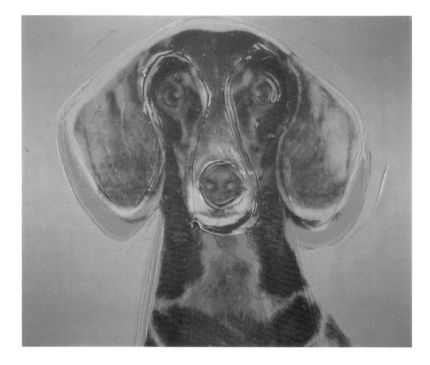

Like Roy Lichtenstein, Andy Warhol was a leading member of the pop art movement. His early work was made up of repeated images of objects and people that Warhol felt were symbols of the U.S. in the 1950s and 1960s—Coke™ bottles, soup cans, dollar bills, and movie stars such as Marilyn Monroe, for example.

Warhol fought against the idea that a work of art should be unique and handmade. One of his favorite techniques was silk-screen printing. It allowed him to make many prints of his work, mimicking the mass production of consumer goods. Before becoming an artist Warhol worked for an advertising agency. In *Portrait of Maurice* the bright, artificial colors of a dachshund dog grab the viewer's attention, just like an advertisement on a billboard or in a magazine.

GLOSSARY OF ART TERMS

ABSTRACT ART
Art that does not represent a subject realistically but that expresses meaning through colors and shapes.

ABSTRACT EXPRESSIONISM
An art movement from the 1940s and 1950s. The abstract expressionists often painted with great energy and boldness as a way of expressing their feelings through paint.

ACRYLIC PAINT
A quick-drying type of paint that was developed in the 1960s. It can be applied as large, flat areas of color or as a thick texture.

CANVAS
A strong cotton fabric used as a painting surface. The canvas is stretched over a frame and then coated with a primer to stop the material from soaking up too much paint.

COLLAGE
A collection of materials, such as paper, fabric, and photographs, stuck onto a surface—and sometimes combined with drawing or painting—to make an image.

COMPOSITION
The arrangement of objects, shapes, and colors in a painting or drawing.

CUBISM
An art movement started around 1907 by Pablo Picasso and Georges Braque. They broke away from the idea that art should copy what can be seen from a single point of view. Cubist paintings and collages are made up of geometric shapes such as cubes, cylinders, and cones.

ETCHING
A picture cut into a metal plate, from which multiple copies can be printed.

EXPRESSIONISM
An early 20th-century art style in which artists used bold brush strokes, distorted shapes, and strong colors to express their emotions rather than show what something really looked like.

IMPRESSIONISM
An art movement that developed in France around 1870. The impressionists tried to capture the atmosphere of scenes rather than record their realistic details. The name comes from Claude Monet's painting *Impression—Sunrise*.

OIL PAINT
Powdered pigments (the color) mixed into an oil-based liquid such as linseed oil. Oil paint dries slowly, leaving the brush strokes visible.

PALETTE KNIFE
A flexible blade used for mixing paint or to lay paint onto a surface very thickly.

PASTEL
Powdered pigment held together by a weak glue and sold in sticks.

PERSPECTIVE
A way of drawing that helps a two-dimensional (flat) picture appear three-dimensional. Faraway objects appear to be smaller than those in the foreground.

POINTILLISM
A technique of using small dots of pure color to build up a painting. From a distance the dots fuse together to create a misty overall effect. Georges Seurat was the first artist to use this technique, which he called divisionism.

POP ART
An art movement from the late 1950s to the early 1970s that celebrated the brash, colorful world of popular culture.

PORTRAIT
A picture of a real person or a group of real people. Portraits can be painted, drawn, printed, sculpted, or photographed.

POSTIMPRESSIONISM
A label describing the work of a group of mostly French artists in the 1880s and 1890s. The postimpressionists learned from the impressionists but then developed their ideas in different ways.

PRIMARY COLORS
The primary colors—red, blue, and yellow—are colors that cannot be made by mixing other colors together. By mixing together the primary colors, however, you can make secondary colors—blue and yellow make green, and red and yellow make orange. Adding black and white creates the tones of the colors.

SILK-SCREEN PRINTING
A method of making prints. First stencils, paint, wax, or photographic chemicals are used to block out areas of an image on a fine mesh screen. Ink is then forced through the screen onto a surface, creating a print.

STILL LIFE
A painting or drawing of a static object or group of static objects such as fruit, flowers, or utensils.

SURREALISM
An art movement popular in the 1920s and 1930s. The surrealists were fascinated by dreams and the way in which people's subconscious minds work. They made bizarre, detailed images that conjure up strange feelings in the viewer.

TRIPTYCH
A painting in three parts. Triptychs are often found in churches above the altar.

The world-renowned City Gallery of Modern Art was founded in 1993 by Ivor Fortune, a millionaire rock star, actor, and adventurer. Over the last three decades Mr. Fortune has traveled around the world to assemble this ambitious collection of modern art masterpieces. Highlights include the atmospheric impressionist works of Claude Monet and Georges Seurat, the energetic drip paintings of Jackson Pollock, and the playful pop art of Andy Warhol and David Hockney. This catalog contains more than 30 of the gallery's best-loved paintings—alongside descriptions of each work—the perfect introduction to modern art!

Inspiration City

CONTEMPLATION

SUN DISK

SEA SONG

THE TRIANGLE

THE LOOKOUT

GAZING

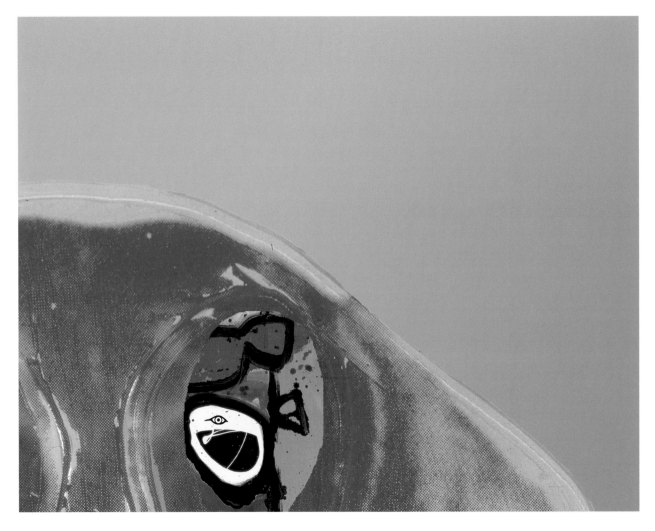

BIRD CALL

WHIRLPOOL

THE BURDEN

DUSK

AFLOAT

PROPHECY

FAREWELL

CLOUDBURST

FRAIL FLAGS

SKY SCAPE

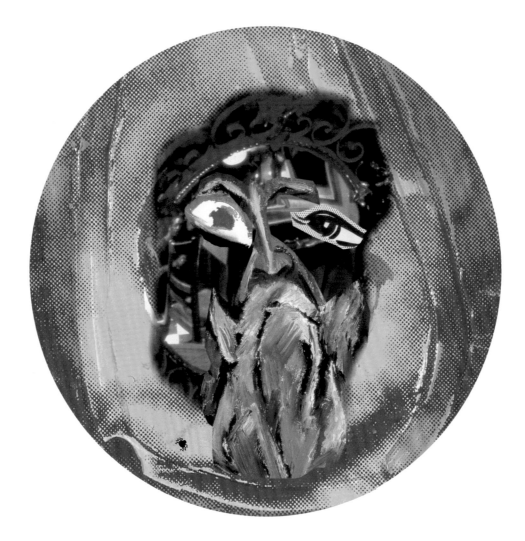

THE STAGE

MISTY MORNING

BELL RINGER

BEACHED

THUNDERSTORM

MOON SONG

MY CASTLE

MUSICIANS

BLACK FAN

THE WATCHER

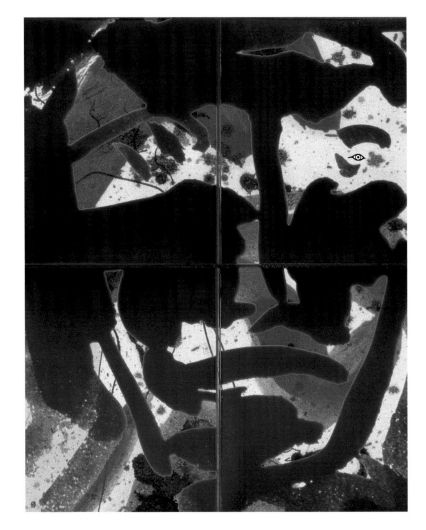

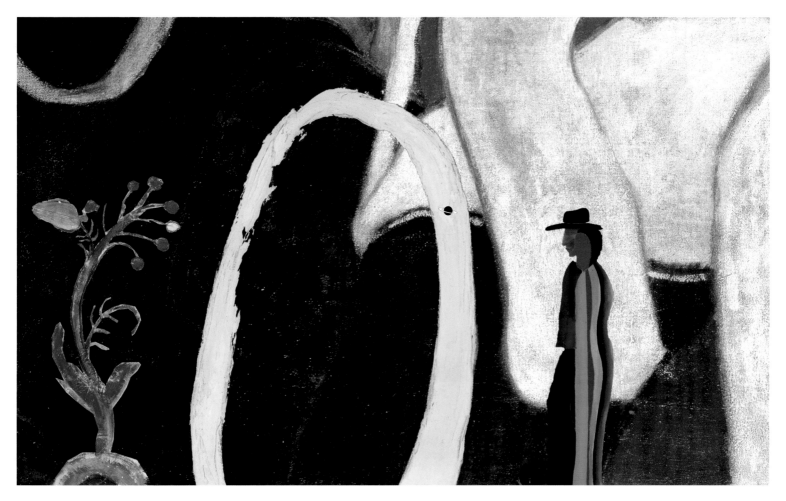

Inspiration City

OCTOBER 1—JANUARY 31

An exhibition of 32 new paintings inspired by the modern art masterpieces of the City Gallery

The gallery would like to thank the 16 artists whose outstanding paintings promise to make *Inspiration City* the art event of the year.

Vernon Venus

Belinda Blinker

Randall Redback

Iris Brown

Sami Saturn

Pluto Moo

Pedro Pupilio

Celia Webb

Tyler Trapdoor

Win Widow

Baxter Ball

Cherry Chambers

Hans van Mars

Victor Vessel

Beat Basham

Petula Pulse

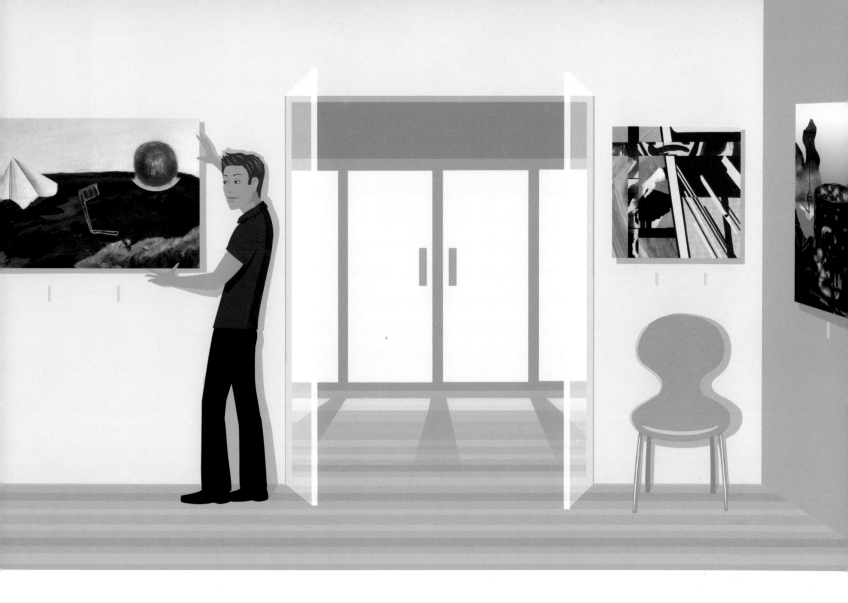

A HELPING HAND

Have you examined every picture from top to bottom? Do you know which artist made each picture, and have you spotted the rogue painting? Perhaps you want to go back and look at the paintings one more time? Try spotting the team symbol first and then look for the details. Remember that there should be only two paintings in each box on your chart—if there are more, you may have missed some details.

45

If you're still stuck, help is here! I cut short my meeting with Mr. Dempsey and have begun to draw my own chart. If you need to compare notes, feel free to check my list.

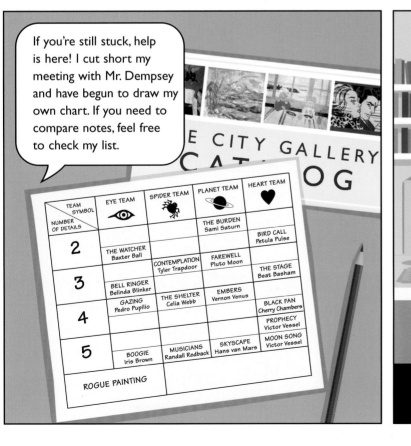

TEAM SYMBOL / NUMBER OF DETAILS	EYE TEAM	SPIDER TEAM	PLANET TEAM	HEART TEAM
2			THE BURDEN Sami Saturn	
	THE WATCHER Baxter Ball			BIRD CALL Petula Pulse
3		CONTEMPLATION Tyler Trapdoor	FAREWELL Pluto Moon	THE STAGE Beat Basham
	BELL RINGER Belinda Blinker		EMBERS Vernon Venus	
4	GAZING Pedro Pupilio	THE SHELTER Celia Webb		BLACK FAN Cherry Chambers
				PROPHECY Victor Vessel
5			SKYSCAPE Hans van Mars	MOON SONG Victor Vessel
	BOOGIE Iris Brown	MUSICIANS Randall Redback		
ROGUE PAINTING				

Finally, when you have completed the chart and figured out who made each picture, I can write the new information labels. And did you find the rogue painting? I hope so—because the future of the gallery rests in your hands.

Turn to pages 46–48 to see if you have succeeded in saving the exhibition!

THE MOMENT OF TRUTH

CONTEMPLATION

TYLER TRAPDOOR 🕷

3 details:
- ● Seurat
- ○ Gauguin
- ○ Nicholson

SUN DISK

PETULA PULSE ♥

2 details:
- ● Hockney
- ○ Nash

SEA SONG

IRIS BROWN 👁

5 details:
- ● Hockney
- ● Frost
- ○ Davie
- ○ Currie
- ○ Penrose

EYE SPY

BAXTER BALL 👁

2 details:
- ● Warhol
- ○ Davie

BIRD CALL

PETULA PULSE ♥

2 details:
- ● Bellany
- ○ Redpath

WHIRLPOOL

PEDRO PUPILIO 👁

4 details:
- ● Penrose
- ○ Frost
- ○ Nolde
- ● Piper

THE BURDEN

SAMI SATURN 🪐

2 details:
- ● Gauguin
- ○ Goncharova

BOOGIE

IRIS BROWN 👁

5 details:
- ● Tanguy
- ● Sutherland
- ○ Penrose
- ○ Davie
- ○ Hockney

FAREWELL

PLUTO MOON 🪐

3 details:
- ● Nolde
- ○ Sutherland
- ○ Cadell

CLOUDBURST

HANS VAN MARS 🪐

5 details:
- ● Tanguy
- ● Currie
- ○ Auerbach
- ○ **Constable**
- ○ Gilbert & George

46

THE TRIANGLE

TYLER TRAPDOOR 🐛

3 details:
- Goncharova
- Davie
- Redpath

THE LOOKOUT

WIN WIDOW 🐛

2 details:
- Eardley
- Lewis

GAZING

PEDRO PUPILIO 👁

4 details:
- Piper
- Bellany
- Cadell
- Colvin

THE SHELTER

CELIA WEBB 🐛

4 details:
- Penrose
- Nash
- Hopper
- Nolan

DUSK

BEAT BASHAM ♥

3 details:
- Nash
- Seurat
- Gauguin

AFLOAT

SAMI SATURN 🪐

2 details:
- Pollock
- Frost

PROPHECY

VICTOR VESSEL ♥

5 details:
- Goncharova
- Nicholson
- Gauguin
- Nolde
- Eardley

47

FRAIL FLAGS

WIN WIDOW 🐛

2 details:
- Tanguy
- Sutherland

SKY SCAPE

HANS VAN MARS 🪐

5 details:
- Van Gogh
- Nicholson
- Seurat
- Nash
- Cézanne

FATHER TIME

RANDALL REDBACK 🐛

5 details:
- Warhol
- Lichtenstein
- Colvin
- Goncharova
- Nolan

THE STAGE

BEAT BASHAM ♥

3 details:
- Kirchner
- Eardley
- van Gogh

MISTY MORNING

BELINDA BLINKER

3 details:
- Nicholson
- Auerbach
- Sutherland

BELL RINGER

BELINDA BLINKER

3 details:
- Currie
- Degas
- Colvin

BEACHED

CELIA WEBB

4 details:
- Hopper
- Seurat
- Frost
- Nolan

THUNDERSTORM

PLUTO MOON

3 details:
- Monet
- Nicholson
- Davie

MOON SONG

VICTOR VESSEL ♥

5 details:
- Redpath
- Kirchner
- Pollock
- Lichtenstein
- Monet

MY CASTLE

CHERRY CHAMBERS ♥

4 details:
- Cézanne
- Hopper
- Piper
- Nolan

MUSICIANS

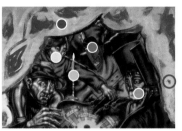

RANDALL REDBACK

5 details:
- Kirchner
- Lewis
- Currie
- Cadell
- Colvin

EMBERS

VERNON VENUS

4 details:
- Tanguy
- Lewis
- Currie
- Colvin

BLACK FAN

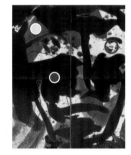

CHERRY CHAMBERS ♥

4 details:
- Gilbert & George
- Cadell
- Warhol
- Lichtenstein

THE WATCHER

BAXTER BALL

2 details:
- Gilbert & George
- Pollock

GOLDEN ARCH

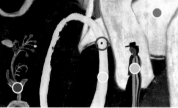

VERNON VENUS

4 details:
- Redpath
- Hockney
- Piper
- Gauguin

48

Congratulations! You've matched the paintings to the artists and saved the exhibition! With just half an hour to spare, all the information panels are in position, and I've taken down the rogue painting—it was *Cloudburst* by Hans van Mars. Now the gallery's reputation is safe, and it looks like the show will be a big success—and it's all thanks to you!

GOOD-BYE!